BEAST
HANK McCOY

MARVEL GIRL
JEAN GREY

CYCLOPS
SCOTT SUMMERS

ANGEL
WARREN WORTHINGTON III

ICEMAN
BOBBY DRAKE

W9-AFH-466

ALL-DIFFERENT

BRIAN MICHAEL
BENDIS
WRITER

STUART
IMMONEN
PENCILER, #18

WADE VON
GRAWBADGER
INKER, #18

BRANDON
PETERSON
WITH MAHMUD ASRAR (#20)
ARTISTS, #19-21

MARTE
GRACIA
COLORIST, #18 & #20

ISRAEL
SILVA
COLORIST, #19-21

VC'S CORY
PETIT
LETTERER

XANDER
JAROWEY
ASSISTANT EDITOR

JORDAN D.
WHITE
ASSOCIATE EDITOR

NICK
LOWE
EDITOR

COVER ART: **BRANDON PETERSON**

X-MEN: GOLD #1

WRITERS: **CHRIS CLAREMONT, STAN LEE & LOUISE SIMONSON, LEN WEIN** AND **FABIAN NICIEZA**
ARTISTS: **BOB McLEOD, WALTER SIMONSON & BOB WIACEK, JORGE MOLINA** AND **SALVADOR LARROCA**
COLORISTS: **ISRAEL SILVA, ANDRES MOSSA** AND **DAVID OCAMPO**
LETTERER: **TOM ORZECHOWSKI**
COVER ART: **OLIVIER COIPEL**
ASSOCIATE EDITORS: **TOM BRENNAN** & **JORDAN D. WHITE**
EDITOR: **NICK LOWE**

COLLECTION EDITOR: **JENNIFER GRÜNWALD** ASSISTANT EDITOR: **SARAH BRUNSTAD**
ASSOCIATE MANAGING EDITOR: **ALEX STARBUCK** EDITOR, SPECIAL PROJECTS: **MARK D. BEAZLEY**
SENIOR EDITOR, SPECIAL PROJECTS: **JEFF YOUNGQUIST** SVP PRINT, SALES & MARKETING: **DAVID GABRIEL**
BOOK DESIGNER: **RODOLFO MURAGUCHI**

EDITOR IN CHIEF: **AXEL ALONSO** CHIEF CREATIVE OFFICER: **JOE QUESADA**
PUBLISHER: **DAN BUCKLEY** EXECUTIVE PRODUCER: **ALAN FINE**

X-MEN CREATED BY STAN LEE & JACK KIRBY

ALL-NEW X-MEN VOL. 4: ALL-DIFFERENT. Contains material originally published in magazine form as ALL-NEW X-MEN #18-21 and X-MEN: GOLD #1. First printing 2014. ISBN# 978-0-7851-8861-2. Published by MARVEL WORLDWIDE, INC., a subsidiary of MARVEL ENTERTAINMENT, LLC. OFFICE OF PUBLICATION: 135 West 50th Street, New York, NY 10020. Copyright © 2013 and 2014 Marvel Characters, Inc. All rights reserved. All characters featured in this issue and the distinctive names and likenesses thereof, and all related indicia are trademarks of Marvel Characters, Inc. No similarity between any of the names, characters, persons, and/or institutions in this magazine with those of any living or dead person or institution is intended, and any such similarity which may exist is purely coincidental. **Printed in the U.S.A.** ALAN FINE, EVP - Office of the President, Marvel Worldwide, Inc. and EVP & CMO Marvel Characters B.V.; DAN BUCKLEY, Publisher & President - Print, Animation & Digital Divisions; JOE QUESADA, Chief Creative Officer; TOM BREVOORT, SVP of Publishing; DAVID BOGART, SVP of Operations & Procurement, Publishing; C.B. CEBULSKI, SVP of Creator & Content Development; DAVID GABRIEL, SVP Print, Sales & Marketing; JIM O'KEEFE, VP of Operations & Logistics; DAN CARR, Executive Director of Publishing Technology; SUSAN CRESPI, Editorial Operations Manager; ALEX MORALES, Publishing Operations Manager; STAN LEE, Chairman Emeritus. For information regarding advertising in Marvel Comics or on Marvel.com, please contact Niza Disla, Director of Marvel Partnerships, at ndisla@marvel.com. For Marvel subscription inquiries, please call 800-217-9158. **Manufactured between 10/24/2014 and 12/1/2014 by R.R. DONNELLEY, INC., SALEM, VA, USA.**

10 9 8 7 6 5 4 3 2 1

Born with genetic mutations that gave them abilities beyond those of normal humans, mutants are the next stage in evolution. As such, they are feared and hated by humanity. A group of mutants known as the X-Men fight for peaceful coexistence between mutants and humankind. But not all mutants see peaceful coexistence as a reality.

ALL·NEW X·MEN

Despite the future Brotherhood of Evil's best efforts, the All-New X-Men cannot return to their original time. Kitty Pryde, the only member of the Jean Grey school who stood up for the All-New X-Men's right to make their own decision about returning to the past, felt betrayed by her teammates and left, deciding to join Cyclops and the Uncanny X-Men at the New Xavier School. Feeling an allegiance to their professor, the All-New X-Men joined her...

WEAPON X! THE LAST PLACE ON THE FACE OF THE EARTH WOLVERINE WOULD LOOK FOR YOU.

NOT BAD, RIGHT?

THAT'S WHY YOU'RE SCOTT SUMMERS.

I HAVE MY MOMENTS.

WHAT IS WEAPON X?

YEARS AGO, AND NOT AS MANY AS YOU WOULD THINK, THIS FACILITY WAS USED FOR EXPERIMENTS.

HORRIBLE, INHUMANE MEDICAL EXPERIMENTS THAT CAUSED THE DEATH OF DOZENS.

ONE OF THE ONLY SURVIVORS WAS OUR "FRIEND" WOLVERINE.

THAT'S WHERE HE GOT THOSE SHINY CLAWS OF HIS.

THIS FACILITY IS A REMINDER THAT LEFT TO THEIR OWN DEVICES...THERE ARE PEOPLE IN THIS WORLD WHO TREAT OTHERS AS NOTHING BUT ANIMALS.

SO...

YOU GOT A GOOD DEAL ON THE RENT?

HOW IS ALL OF THIS GOING TO WORK, EXACTLY?

STUDENTS, WHY DON'T WE TAKE THE ORIGINAL X-MEN TO THEIR NEW LIVING QUARTERS.

LET'S MAKE THEM ALL FEEL AT HOME.

WE'VE TRAVELED FROM THE PAST TO LIVE IN A RENOVATED MUTANT TORTURE CHAMBER, LADIES AND GENTLEMEN.

DR. MCCOY, IT IS AN HONOR.

UH YEAH, HI.

WHERE ARE YOU TAKING US NOW?

THEY'RE TIRED.

WE'VE ALL BEEN THROUGH A LOT.

LET THEM SLEEP.

YEAH YEAH...

ALL RIGHT...

WHY DON'T YOU GO DO THE SAME, SLIM?

PLEASE, DON'T *CALL* ME THAT.

SORRY.

YOU MADE THE RIGHT CHOICE BRINGING THEM HERE, KATYA.

WE'LL SEE.

I'M SORRY YOU AND YOUR BOYFRIEND BROKE--

IT'S NOT YOUR FAULT, LITTLE ONE. HOMO SAPIENS ARE THE ONLY *TRUE* WORK OF GOD.

NO!

GOD DOESN'T WANT MUTANTS. HE GAVE THE GARDEN OF EDEN TO HUMANS.

THIS IS THE JUDGMENT DAY.

I'M *NOT* MUTANT!

KRAKOOM

HOW DARE YOU?!

WOW.

GOD DID NOT CREATE MUTANT.

SURE, HE DID.

SEE?

"YE SERPENTS, YE GENERATION OF VIPERS...

"HOW CAN YE ESCAPE THE DAMNATION OF HELL?"

WHY?

WHY DO YOU THINK I'M A MUTANT?

"THY KINGDOM COME, THY WILL BE DONE, ON EARTH AS IT IS IN HEAVEN!"

"THY KINGDOM COME, THY WILL BE DOAAAAGGHH!"

HERE'S WHAT I DON'T UNDERSTAND...

HELP ME OUT HERE.

YOU'RE THE DEVIL.

WEEEOOOOEEEOOOOEEEEEEOOWW

THE POLICE ARE HERE, THAT MEANS IT'S TIME TO GO.

NO. NO WE DON'T RUN.

WE'RE THE GOOD GUYS.

THE POLICE WILL NEED A STATEMENT.

REALLY? A STATEMENT?

YOU THINK THEY WANT A STATEMENT?

FROM YOU?

ON THE GROUND!

DON'T EVEN THINK ABOUT IT, MUTANT!

HANDS ON YOUR HEAD AND YOUR FACE ON THE GROUND!

STOP RUNNING! WHY ARE YOU RUNNING FROM ME?!

NO!

COME ON!

REALLY?

STOP!

NYYAAGGH!

HEY, COOL IT!

COME ON!

HEY HEY HEY...YOU CAN'T TOUCH ME.

GET IT?

I CAN DO THIS ALL DAY.

AGHK!

AGGH!

CALM DOWN!

OFF ME!

AGH!

STOP!

SORRY.

SORRY.

ARE YOU OKAY?

YOU ARE FREAKING THE FREAK OUT. DO YOU NOT RECOGNIZE ME?!

GET OFF!

JUST SETTLE-- SETTLE DOWN!

WHAT HAPPENED TO YOU?!

CAN I HELP YOU TWO FINE, FINE LOVELY LLLADIES WITH SUMPTHIN'?

LADIES, LADIES, LADIES!

LITTLE TOO MUCH TO DRINK TONIGHT?

A COUPLE OF HOURS AGO YOU WERE BALD AND SICKLY AND SCARED AND BEING CHASED BY ANTI-MUTANT RELIGIOUS ZEALOTS...

YOU DIDN'T RECOGNIZE OUR PROFESSOR KITTY EVEN THOUGH SHE SAID SHE KNEW YOU.

I FEEL-- I FEEL THIS IS A TRICK.

IT HAS TO BE A TRICK.

WHAT...

WHAT DO YOU WANT FROM ME?! WHAT DOES EVERYBODY WANT FROM ME?!

YOU'RE A MUTANT.

YOU'RE A FRIEND OF OUR FRIENDS.

WE WANT TO HELP YOU.

SCOTT SUMMERS...

AND THAT WAS ACTUALLY THE REAL JEAN GREY.

JEAN GREY.

WOW.

WHAT HAPPENED TO YOU?

DEAR GOD...

I CAN SEE HER THOUGHTS.

I KNOW WHAT HAPPENED TO HER.

IT'S AWFUL

WHAT?

I THINK IT'S JUST ONE OF MY FAMOUS BEING-AT-THE-WRONG-PLACE-AT-THE-WRONG-TIMES.

THEY HATE MUTANTS.

AND THEY COULD SMELL IT ON ME.

I CAN HEAL AND I WAS HEALING FROM AS CLOSE TO DEAD AS I EVER HOPE TO BE.

I WAS HEALING MYSELF FROM ALMOST NOTHING.

THAT'S PROBABLY WHY I WAS HAVING TROUBLE SEEING YOU ALL FOR WHAT YOU WERE.

I WAS OUT OF MY HEAD.

ALL THINGS BEING EQUAL, I'D LIKE TO FIND THOSE PURIFIERS AND TAKE OUT MY HALF-MISPLACED ANGER AND MY ACTUAL ANGER ON THEM.

DO YOU KNOW WHERE THEY ARE?

WHY ARE YOU ALL LIVING IN WEAPON X?

WE WERE TOLD IT WAS THE LAST PLACE ANYBODY WOULD LOOK FOR US.

WHO TOLD YOU THAT?

ME.

"THAT MEANS THEY ARE BREAKING THE RULES OF TIME AND SPACE AS IF THESE RULES DON'T APPLY TO THEM.

"AS IF THEIR NEEDS ARE MORE IMPORTANT THAN OURS.

FOR THEY ARE OUR BURNING BUSH.

THE ORIGINAL X-MEN, WHO LAST NIGHT FELLED *MANY* OF OUR PURIFIER BROTHERS, ARE LIVING IN THE NOW?!

WHAT ARE THEY *DOING* HERE?

"YOU DON'T HAVE TO BE A SCIENTIST TO KNOW THAT IF THEY ARE HERE INSTEAD OF WHERE THEY *BELONG*, THEN OUR FUTURE, THE FUTURE OF OUR CHILDREN, IS IN *DANGER*.

"WE COULD VERY WELL CEASE TO EXIST BECAUSE OF THEIR SELFISH ACTIONS."

JUST BECAUSE THEY HAVE THE POWER TO DO SOMETHING DOESN'T MEAN IT IS SOMETHING THEY SHOULD BE *ALLOWED* TO DO.

THERE ARE CONSEQUENCES.

A HUMAN BEING WOULD UNDERSTAND THAT.

A CHILD OF GOD WOULD UNDERSTAND THAT.

I PRAYED TO GOD IN HEAVEN ABOVE FOR A SIGN OF PROOF THAT THE MUTANT MUST BE DESTROYED...

AND HE BROUGHT THE ORIGINAL MUTANTS HERE TO US.

HE GAVE US A--

SO, JUST FYI, THEY KNOW WE'RE HERE.

AW, YOU CAN STICK YOUR ARM IN ELECTRICAL THINGS AND ZAATT-- THAT IS COOL.

THANK YOU.

AS WE PRACTICED.

EVERYONE FOLLOW LAURA BUT EVERYONE ANSWER TO SCOTT.

LISTEN FOR JEAN'S VOICE IN YOUR HEAD.

SHE WILL LET YOU KNOW WHEN IT'S TIME. WE ARE RIGHT BEHIND YOU.

GOD JUST TOLD ME THAT...

...HE WANTS US ALL TO GET NAKED.

WHAT ARE YOU TALKING ABOUT?

WHAT'S WRONG WITH YOU?

MAYBE IT IS THEM.

YA THINK?

X-MEN, GO GET 'EM.

ABOMINATION!

AGH!

NYYAAGGH!

NNGGG!

NICE JOB, X-MEN.

LET'S WRAP THIS UP FAST.

HANK, GO GET WARREN.

EVERYONE RETREAT NOW!

SLICE

HRRAAGH!

SLICE

OH NO.

I THINK WE HAVE THIS!

NO!

GOD'S WILL BE DONE.

21

OKAY... NO SMALL TALK.

WE HAVE BEEN BRIEFED AND WE HAVE GONE OVER YOUR SON'S MEDICAL FILES.

THAT'S WHY WE'RE HERE.

I WILL BE FRANK, I AM OF TWO MINDS ON THIS.

GOD CREATED MAN.

HIS WILL BE DONE.

GOD ALSO CREATED SCIENCE.

I APPRECIATE THAT AS WELL.

WOULDN'T IT BE IRONIC IF HE TURNED OUT TO BE A MUTANT?

WE CAN SAVE YOUR BOY AND WE WILL CREATE WITHIN HIM THE POWER TO FIGHT YOUR CAUSE.

NOW... THERE IS THE UGLY TOPIC OF REMUNERATION.

WHATEVER IT TAKES.

TODAY.

LET US PRAY.

"BELOVED, DO NOT BELIEVE EVERY SPIRIT...

"BUT TEST THE SPIRITS TO SEE WHETHER THEY ARE FROM GOD.

"FOR MANY FALSE PROPHETS HAVE GONE OUT INTO THE WORLD.

"BY THIS YOU KNOW THE SPIRIT OF GOD: EVERY SPIRIT THAT CONFESSES THAT JESUS CHRIST HAS COME IN THE FLESH IS FROM GOD.

"AND EVERY SPIRIT THAT DOES NOT CONFESS THAT JESUS HAS COME, IS NOT FROM GOD.

"THIS IS THE SPIRIT OF THE ANTICHRIST, WHICH YOU HEARD WAS COMING AND NOW IS IN THE WORLD ALREADY.

"LITTLE CHILDREN, YOU ARE FROM GOD AND HAVE OVERCOME THEM.

"FOR HE WHO IS IN YOU IS GREATER THAN HE WHO IS IN THE WORLD.

"THEY ARE FROM THE WORLD, THEREFORE THEY SPEAK FROM THE WORLD, AND THE WORLD LISTENS TO THEM."

NOW LET'S GUT THESE &#$% SONS OF SATAN.

NO!

WAIT.

STRYKER, YOU--YOU SAID THESE ARE THE ORIGINAL X-MEN.

FROM THE PAST. THAT THEY, WHAT? TIME TRAVELED HERE?

OBVIOUSLY.

SO, LIKE, IF WE KILL THEM DOESN'T THAT CREATE A PARADOX?

I MEAN, LIKE IN THE MOVIES, WOULDN'T THERE BE LIKE A--A--

A BUTTERFLY EFFECT.

YES. LIKE, MAYBE SO MUCH WOULD CHANGE THAT WE WOULDN'T EVEN EXIST OR SOMETHING.

OR WE *KILL* THEM AND THE ENTIRE MUTANT CAUSE IS *HOBBLED* BECAUSE THE ORIGINAL X-MEN NEVER HAD THE PRESENCE THEY ONCE HAD.

AND THAT'S *MORE* THAN WE COULD HAVE HOPED FOR.

GOD'S WILL BE DONE.

BUT-- BUT, HOLD ON!

JUST, I MEAN, THERE'S A LOT RIDING ON THIS.

THIS MUTANT KILLED MY FATHER.

A MUTANT KILLED MY WIFE.

BUT--BUT THEY DID IT WITH TRICKERY.

THIS--WE DON'T KNOW WHERE THEY ARE FROM OR WHY THEY ARE HERE.

WE DON'T KNOW *WHAT* WILL HAPPEN.

GOD BROUGHT THEM HERE FOR A REASON.

BUT-- BUT--

IS THERE SOMEONE WE COULD TALK TO ABOUT THIS?

SOMEONE SMARTER THAN US.

SPASSHH

RRR!!

MMAAARR!!

CLINK

CLINK

SNIKT

COME ON, THEN!!

ALL RIGHT...

WHERE DID YOU--?

WHERE DID WE *GET* THIS? IS *THAT* WHAT YOU WERE GOING TO ASK?

DO YOU *REALLY* NOT KNOW THAT THIS SHOW OF YOURS WAS BROADCAST ALL OVER THE WORLD?

THE ENTIRE WORLD SAW WHAT A MONSTER YOU ARE.

YOU REALLY DIDN'T KNOW.

YOU WERE ON A REALITY SHOW. YOU WERE POPCORN FOR MORONS.

I WONDER IF THE REST OF THESE MISPLACED MONSTERS YOU RUN AROUND WITH KNOW WHAT YOU ARE CAPABLE OF...

LET'S GO FIND OUT.

IS HE AWAKE?

I'M AWAKE.

WHY ARE YOU HERE, SCOTT SUMMERS?

I'M HAPPY TO LEAVE.

WHY ARE YOU HERE IN *THIS TIME?*

I'D LIKE TO TALK TO MY LAWYER.

HELP HIM REMEMBER.

NYAAGGH!

DR. STRYKER, A.I.M. IS HERE.

I'M DR. MONICA RAPPACCINI, OF A.I.M.

YOU CALLED?

THAT IS KITTY PRYDE.

AND THAT--

IS THAT?

YES.

THAT IS JEAN GREY.

JEAN GREY IS DEAD.

THAT IS HER.

COME HERE FROM THE PAST.

THE PAST?

SHE LOOKS SO YOUNG.

SEVENTEEN?

IS THIS REAL?

THEY ATTACKED US AND WE WERE ABOUT TO EXECUTE THEM IN THE NAME OF--

YOU'LL DO NO SUCH THING.

BECAUSE IT WOULD CAUSE A PARADOX.

THAT'S THE BEST THING IT COULD DO.

SO I SHOULD LET THEM GO?!

YOU SHOULD LET THEM GO, BURN THIS PLACE TO THE GROUND, MOVE TO AUCKLAND, NEW ZEALAND AND START OVER AND HOPE THEY NEVER FIND YOU.

THAT IS UNACCEPTABLE.

SO IS REALITY TURNING ITSELF INSIDE OUT.

LISTEN, YOU AND I, SINCE YOU WERE A CHILD... A.I.M. AND THE PURIFIERS HAVE HAD A LONG-STANDING AND FRUITFUL RELATIONSHIP...

WE SELL YOU OUR BEST WEAPONS AND YOU DO WHAT YOU THINK YOU NEED TO DO.

BUT HEAR ME NOW...

YOU CALLED ME DOWN HERE FOR THE *EXPERT OPINION* OF A.I.M. AND I HAVE *GIVEN IT TO YOU.*

PULL THE PLUG ON THIS NOW.

THEN THEY WIN!!

NOW HOLD ON A MINUTE...

SCOTT?

THAT ISN'T TO SAY THEY CAN'T BE OF USE.

GARY, GET ME MY BAG.

SCOTT?!

CAN YOU HEAR MY THOUGHTS?

WHAT ARE YOU GOING TO DO?

SOME DNA GATHERING.

MY COLLEAGUES AND I ARE WORKING ON SOME INTERESTING EXPERIMENTS.

BOBBY?

HANK?

WHAT?

I DIDN'T SAY ANYTHING, MUTIE.

WE STARTED WORK ON A PROCESS THAT WOULD ELIMINATE THE MUTANT GENE--

RIIIIPP

BUT WITH THE GROWING NUMBER OF TERRIGENESIS INHUMANS POPPING UP ALL OVER THE WORLD...

LAURA?

NO! NO! STAY OUT OF MY MIND!

WE'VE BEEN CREATING SOME REALLY INTERESTING DNA SPLICING.

YOU ARE TAKING *THESE* ABOMINATIONS AND *THOSE* ABOMINATIONS AND MAKING *MORE* ABOMINATIONS?

YOU KNOW WHAT?

WHEN WE'RE DONE HERE YOU *CAN* KILL THIS ONE.

LOOK AT HER!

SHE'S ALL GROWN UP. THIS IS *OUR* KITTY PRYDE.

YOU CAN KILL *HER* WITHOUT CAUSING A CONTINUUM DISASTER.

ARE YOU OKAY, MR. STRYKER?

I'M--I'M PRAYING.

I READ YOUR GENETIC FILE ON MY WAY DOWN HERE.

HOW ARE YOU FEELING?

HEADACHES?

FINE.

SOMETIMES.

TROUBLE SLEEPING?

I *DON'T* SLEEP.

THAT'S NOT GOOD.

AND ANYWAY, IT'S NOT LIKE--

OOPS!

I WANT YOU TO COME VISIT ME AT THE A.I.M. COMPOUND NEXT WEEK...

I HAVE SOME INTERESTING NEW IMPLANTS THAT I THINK WOULD LEVEL YOU OFF QUITE WELL.

THERE'S BEEN A LOT OF ADVANCEMENTS SINCE MY PREDECESSOR WORKED HIS MAGIC ON YOU.

THERE'S LITERALLY NO REASON YOU SHOULD *NOT* COME IN FOR A TUNE-UP.

NOO!!

AAGGHH!!

AAGGH!!

BOY! YOU ARE AN EMBARRASSMENT!

WHAT DID THEY DO TO YOU?

MARIA HILL, PLEASE...

NEXT: THE TRIAL OF JEAN GREY

Welcome X-Fans,

When I was 12 years old, sitting in a hospital bed after breaking my arm, my brother Matt brought me a brown paper bag full of X-Men comics and changed my life. While I waited for my arm to heal, I read X-MEN #13 and CLASSIC X-MEN #14 and my mind was blown. A nerdy choirboy on the west side of Cleveland found solace in the strangest heroes of all and the X-Men have been a part of my life ever since.

It is with great pride that I welcome you to this very special issue commemorating 50 years of the X-Men. It is truly an honor that so many of the most important creators in the X-Men's publishing history were able to join in on this. First of all, the grand poo-bah of the Marvel Universe and co-creator of the X-Men, STAN LEE, was gracious enough to script a story starring the original five X-Men! Joining him are LOUISE and WALTER SIMONSON, who helped bring Cyclops, Marvel Girl, Iceman, Angel and the Beast back together in X-FACTOR many years later (in addition to Louise's long run as X-Men Editor!).

There's also a story by former Marvel Editor-In-Chief and second man ever to write the X-Men, ROY THOMAS. Roy is joined by PAT OLLIFFE for an off-beat story staring BANSHEE and SUNFIRE before they joined the X-Men!

Every X-Fan knows that the comic that started a second life for the X-Men was 1975's GIANT-SIZE X-MEN. The writer of that landmark issue and the co-creator of Wolverine, LEN WEIN is joined here by artist-extraordinaire JORGE MOLINA for a story that takes place right in the middle of GSXM!

FABIAN NICIEZA wrote some of the most popular X-Men stories in the 1990's (including much of the "X-Cutioner's Song" story that made the X-Men an addiction for this X-Editor). Joining him is SALVADOR LARROCA whose runs on X-TREME X-MEN and X-MEN cement him as one of X-Fandom's favorite artists.

But the first story and centerpiece of this volume is by one of the men most responsible for turning the X-Men into the biggest comics franchise of all time--CHRIS CLAREMONT. Chris, alongside some of the greatest artists and story-tellers to ever draw comics, took a book that had been cancelled years before and made it the must-read book that dominated the comic book marketplace for more than a decade. Joining Chris for this story is classic X-Men artist and NEW MUTANTS co-creator BOB MCLEOD!

Lastly, following these classic stories are samples of some current X-Men books that we think readers who may have stopped reading the exploits of the Children of the Atom might enjoy!

Here's to 50 more years!

Nick Lowe
X-Men Senior Editor

I'M **KITTY PRYDE.**

I'M A MUTANT-- AND AN X-MAN.

MOST EVERYONE LOOKS AT ME, THEY SEE A KID, BARELY INTO HER TEENS.

THEY DON'T KNOW I CAN WALK THROUGH WALLS.

THAT I'VE BEEN TO ANOTHER GALAXY AND MET ALIENS. ONE EVEN CAME HOME WITH ME: MY BEST FRIEND LOCKHEED.

THAT I'VE HELPED SAVE THE WORLD, AT LEAST TWICE.

RIGHT NOW, THOUGH, I'M DOING HOMEWORK.

by CHRIS CLAREMONT & BOB McLEOD

ORORO: **STORM**

LOGAN: **WOLVERINE**

KURT: **NIGHTCRAWLER**

PIOTR: **COLOSSUS**

ROGUE

SCOTT: **CYCLOPS**

PRRRRRRR

私はちょうど宇宙を保存するのを助けた

*I just helped save the Universe

TOM ORZECHOWSKI, LETTERER
ISRAEL SILVA, COLORIST
WITH SPECIAL THANKS TO LARRY HAMA

AMONG OTHER THINGS.

IT SO *BITES*, DRAGON—

—WHAT HAPPENED BETWEEN LOGAN AND *LADY MARIKO*.

SHE *LOVED* HIM.

I *KNOW* THAT IN MY BONES.

I *HATE* THE WAY LOGAN ALWAYS SNEAKS UP ON ME.

NO MATTER HOW HARD I TRY, I CAN NEVER *SPOT* HIM.

I GUESS IT REALLY IS TRUE: HE'S THE *BEST* THERE IS AT WHAT HE DOES...

...AND WHAT HE DOES BEST, *ISN'T* VERY NICE.

IT'S A NO-BRAINER THAT WE'LL CHECK THIS OUT, AND LEND A HAND.

THE X-MEN ARE *HEROES*, THAT'S WHAT WE DO.

AND BEING MUTANTS, WHIC[H] MEANS BEING FEARED AN[D] *HATED* BY JUST ABOUT EVERYBODY, IT WOULDN'T H[URT] TO MAKE SOME NEW *FRIEN[DS].*

FIRST OFF, WE MOVE *PROFESSO[R]* AND THE OTHER CIVILIANS UP T[O] WHERE THEY'LL BE SAFE, ABOA[RD] THE *STARJAMMER.*

WE USE HOLOGRAM COMMLINKS AND THE PROF'S TELEPATHY TO STAY IN TOUCH.

IT MUST BE SO *COOL* FOR SCOTT, TO KNOW HIS *DAD (CORSAIR)* IS CAPTAIN OF A *STARSHIP.*

MY DAD'S A *BANKER.*

NONE OF THIS FEELS RIGHT, CHARLES.

WE CAN'T GET DECENT READINGS OF THE SITE. SOME SORT OF *INHIBITER* FIELD IS DISRUPTING OUR SCANS.

I AGREE, *NATHAN.*

DO NOT WORRY, *MADELYNE.* SCOTT WILL BE FINE.

IF YOU SAY SO, *LILANDRA.*

FORGIVE ME, X-MEN, BUT I'M UNABLE TO ACCESS ANY COHERENT THOUGHTS FROM THE CRISIS ZONE. NO ONE THERE SEEMS TO KNOW WHAT'S HAPPENING--

--ONLY THAT IT *TERRIFIES* THEM.

A CLOAKED DISASTER?

THAT DOES NOT SOUND GOOD.

BETTER BE READY FOR ANYTHING *STORM.*

HOW MUCH LONGER, *NIGHT CRAWLER?*

A MATTER OF MINUTES, *MEIN FREUNDE.*

ONE OF US IS A NEW ARRIVAL TO THE X-MEN. IT'S WEIRD LOOKING AT *ROGUE* AS A TEAMMATE, CONSIDERING THAT WHEN WE FIRST MET, SHE TRIED TO KILL US.

BUT LOGAN TRUSTS HER.

PROFESSOR XAVIER SAYS SHE NEEDS OUR HELP.

IN JAPAN, SHE ALMOST DIED HELPING US. SHE'S STILL RECOVERING FROM THOSE WOUNDS BUT SHE WOULDN'T STAY BEHIND.

SHE'S NOT THAT MUCH OLDER THAN ME.

YOU DID GOOD AGAINST THE SILVER SAMURAI AND VIPER.

DON'T TOUCH ME, KITTY--NOT WITH BARE HANDS.

DO THAT, AH ABSORB YOUR POWERS AN' MEMORIES.

YOU CAN'T TURN IT OFF?

AH WISH! THAT'S WHY AH'M ALWAYS FULLY COVERED.

DIDN'T MUCH CARE, B'FORE. AH ALWAYS B'LIEVED THE EFFECT WAS TEMPORARY--

--'TIL I GRABBED *CAROL DANVERS.*

WHAT AH TOOK FROM HER DIDN'T GO BACK.

NOW IT'S LIKE AH GOT HER LIVIN' INSIDE MY SOUL.

AH DON'T WANT TO RISK THAT HAPPENIN' TO ANYONE ELSE, EVER!

THAT REALLY SUCKS.

OH, YEAH!

I'M SORRY, ROGUE-- REALLY.

BUT IF ANYONE CAN HELP, IT'S THE PROFESSOR.

THAT'S WHY AH'M HERE.

FRONT AND CENTER, X-MEN.

WE'RE COMING UP ON OUR TARGET.

YEARGKGH!

AH-- FELT THAT!

TOO MANY ROBOTS-- HITTIN' ME TOO FAST, TOO HARD--

--CAN'T TAKE MUCH MORE--!

SCHILDWACHTER--* --LEAVE MY FRIEND ALONE!

KZANG!

AS I FEARED, ROGUE STILL SUFFERS FROM THE WOUNDS SHE RECEIVED IN JAPAN.

I HAVE TO PROTECT HER.

* "SENTINE IN GERMA

ANY IDEAS, CYCLOPS?

I-- I--!

I CAN'T CONCENTRATE.

I KEEP THINKING OF **MADELYNE.**

SHE'S UNDER ATTACK ABOARD THE STARJAMMER...

...AND THERE'S NOTHING I CAN DO TO HELP!

SCOTT, YOU HAVE TO **FOCUS!**

I KNOW YOU FEAR FOR THE WOMAN YOU **LOVE--**

--BUT RIGHT NOW, IT IS THE **X-MEN** WHO NEED YOU!

X-MEN-- STARJAMMER SENSORS REPORT THAT THESE **NEO-SENTINELS** ARE CONSTANTLY IMPROVING THEMSELVES!

IN SHORT ORDER, THEY WILL DEFEAT US.

WE HAVE TO STOP THEM **NOW,** WHILE W STILL HAVE THE CHANCE.

MAKES ME PROUD.

PIOTR SPINS US HARD.

ADAMANTIUM BLADES CUT OPEN THE ROBOT.

THE INCREDIBLE HEAT INHIBITS ITS REPAIR SYSTEMS.

THAT GIVES ME AN INSTANT TO GRAB HO OF ITS INTERNAL GRID

...AND TEAR IT FRE

BEING INTANGIBLE--IN GHOST-FORM--HELPS PROTECT ME FROM THE HEAT, BUT I STILL HURT.

WITH LOGAN, EVEN AS HE BURNS, HE HEALS, OVER AND OVER AGAIN.

ALL THREE OF US SUFFER.

WE DON'T QU

KITTY HAS MADE THE ROBOTS VULNERABLE.

SCOTT KNOCKS THEM DOWN.

IT IS MY JOB TO FINISH THEM.

MY FRIENDS I WILL NO FAIL YOU

WHEN ALL IS SAID AND DONE, THERE'S NO BIG SPLASH ON THE GLOBAL NEWS NET.

INDUSTRIAL ACCIDENT IN CENTRAL CHINA, YADDA-YADDA-YADDA. NO MENTION OF US OR THE SENTINELS.

JUST LIKE USUAL, THE X-MEN SAVE THE WORLD AND NOBODY NOTICES.

'CEPT US.

SO WE THROW OURSELVES A PARTY.

LIFE CAN BE SO WEIRD--HERE I AM, A KID FROM DEERFIELD, ILLINOIS, AND I'M MORE USED TO FLYING STARSHIPS TO THE FAR END OF CREATION, THAN I AM TO RIDING THE "EL."

SOMEDAY, I FIGURE I'LL HAVE A LIFE, BUT FOR RIGHT NOW--

--I WOULDN'T TRADE THIS FOR ANYTHING!

I'M NOT USE TO SEEING YOU ON YOUR FEET, PROFESSOR.

FOR THE PRESENT, SCOTT, JUST A PSYCHIC ILLUSION.

WHERE ARE THE PROF AND LILANDRA?

NEVER YOU MIND, GIRL.

I CANNOT HELP WONDERING IF THESE SENTINELS ARE A PREMONITION OF THE FUTURE--!

LET THE FUTURE TAKE CARE OF ITSELF, ORORO.

MINE, I HOPE, INVOLVES A HANDSOME MAN REFILLING MY GLASS.

ACTUALLY, I HAD A BETTER IDEA.

WHATEVER COMES, THE X-MEN WILL ALWAYS FIND A WAY TO WIN.

I PRAY YOU ARE RIGHT, CHARLES.

TIME WILL TELL.

I, TOO, KNOW WHAT IT'S LIKE TO BE HUNTED.

I ALSO KNOW, IF MY FAITH MEANS ANY-THING...

...IT IS THAT WE ALL DESERVE A SECOND CHANCE.

WELCOM TO THE X-MEN ROGUE

YOU OKAY?

I'LL SURVIVE.

I KNOW YOU WILL.

YOU DID GOOD AGAINST THE ROBOTS.

JUST FOLLOWING YOUR LEAD, OLD MAN.

FOR AS LONG AS YOU NEED IT...

...I'LL BE HERE TO WATCH YOUR BACK.

TOUGH GIRL, HUH?

YOU BET'CHA!

THAT'S THE WAY IT WAS, THAT'S THE WAY IT IS.

THAT'S THE WAY IT ALWAYS WILL BE.

END

HAH! JUST AS I **SUSPECTED!**

BUT, IN THE TIME SINCE I WAS LAST IN AMERICA, I DARED HOPE THEY WOULD HAVE LEARNED TO LEAVE ME IN **PEACE.**

I'M **NO** X-MAN... THOUGH ME QUARRELS WITH THOSE LADS ARE LONG SINCE UNDER THE SOD.

BUT THEY'VE **NAUGHT** TO DO WITH WHY I'M **HERE.**

I STOPPED OFF IN MEMPHIS TO BE HAVIN' A LOOK AT THE BIRTHPLACE OF **SUN RECORDS,** YONDER.

AND SURE IT IS **YOU** HAD THE SAME PURPOSE-- OR WHY BE HIRING A CAB TO **UNION STREET?**

YOU... ARE RIGHT.

LIKE MANY IN JAPAN, I ADMIT TO A FONDNESS FOR THE MUSIC OF **ELVIS PRESLEY.**

MORE OF A **COUNTRY MUSIC** MAN MESELF...

PERHAPS WE SHOULD DISCUSS OUR VARIOUS CONNECTIONS...OVER A CUP OF TEA.

OR COFFEE. ME BUS DOESN'T LEAVE TILL THE MORN.

BUT SUN, BESIDES YOUNG ELVIS, HAD **JOHNNY CASH...CARL PERKINS...**

...SO NOW YOU UNDER- STAND MY HOSTILITY TO ANYONE I THINK MIGHT BE AN X-MAN.

BUT YE AND ME, WE'RE MERELY **MUTANTS**-- THE **BANSHEE** AND **SUNFIRE!**

...WELL, BE HAVIN' A GOOD FLIGHT HOME TO TOKYO, LADDIE.

AND I HOPE YOU ENJOY YOUR BUS RIDE TO...**NASHVILLE,** WAS IT?

PLEASE-- CALL ME **SHIRO.**

AYE... HOME OF THE **GRAND OL' OPRY!**

XAVIER'S MANSION, ~AY ONE.

GOTTA GIVE BALDIE CREDIT...

HE MANAGED TO TELEPATHICALLY TEACH ENGLISH TO THIS ENTIRE FREAK SHOW IN LESS THAN AN HOUR...

QUESTION IS, HAVE I MADE A MISTAKE DUMPING DEPARTMENT H IN FAVOR OF THIS SQUAD OF SCREWBALLS?

I MEAN, HOW FAR CAN THEY EVEN BE TRUSTED?

EVEN I'M IMPRESSED.

MY FRIENDS, ALLOW ME TO INTRODUCE SCOTT SUMMERS--

--THE MAN CALLED CYCLOPS!

HE WILL FILL YOU IN ON THE DETAILS.

SIMPLY PUT, PEOPLE, YOU ARE HERE BECAUSE-- THE X-MEN HAVE DISAPPEARED!

OPTIONS!

LEN WEIN
WRITER
JORGE MOLINA
ARTIST
TOM ORZECHOWSKI
LETTERER

THEY **VANISHED** ON THE ISLAND OF **KRAKOA** IN THE SOUTH PACIFIC.

WE'RE GOING THERE TO **FIND** THEM, IF THEY'RE STILL **ALIVE**--

--AND WE'RE GOING TO BRING THEM **HOME.**

OF COURSE, SINCE WE'VE NO IDEA WHAT **HAPPENED** TO THE OTHERS, YOU MUST BE PREPARED FOR **ANYTHING**--

--INCLUDING THE POSSIBILITY OF HAVING TO **FIGHT** YOUR OWN BROTHERS IN BLOOD.

GOOD **POINT.** HOW **WOULD** I DEAL WITH THIS CROWD IF I HAD TO TAKE 'EM **DOWN?**

AIN'T **CRAZY** ABOUT THE IDEA--BUT I OUGHT'A BE **PREPARED.**

OKAY, LET'S START WITH **IRISH** OVER THERE...

BANSHEE'S **SONIC POWERS** ARE ALL IN HIS **THROAT**--

--SO A QUICK **CLAW** TO THE **VOCAL CORDS**--

--AND PROBLEM **SOLVED.**

SAME GOES FOR **SUMMERS.**

FOR ALL HIS **POWER,** I CAN STILL TAKE HIM **DOWN** WITH A POKE IN THE EYE WITH A **SHARP STICK.**

'S BRUTAL--

--BUT EFFICIENT.

DON'T THINK I'D HAVE TO BE *QUITE* AS TOUGH ON WHAT'S-'IS-NAME, *THUNDERBIRD.*

HE'S STRONG, QUICK, AGILE--

HE'S BASICALLY ME WITHOUT ALL THE *COOL* POWERS.

--BUT HE AIN'T GOT A TENTH OF THE *COMBAT EXPERIENCE* I HAVE.

HE MAY COME AT ME *HARD*-- AND THAT'S JUST THE WAY HE'S GOING *DOWN.*

KAY--

--SO THAT'S *THREE* DOWN.

THE RUSSKIE--*COLOSSUS*-- LOOKS LIKE A BLOCK OF SOLID *MUSCLE*--

--AND HIS ABILITY TO *TRANSFORM* THAT BULK INTO *METAL* MAKES HIM *FORMIDABLE*--

--BUT WHEN IT COMES DOWN TO STEEL VERSUS *ADAMANTIUM*--

--IT'S REALLY NO *CONTEST!*

OKAY, SO THAT LEAVES THE SELF-RIGHTEOUS SAMURAI SUNFIRE...

I AM NOT *CERTAIN* ABOUT THIS, XAVIER.

THE FILE ON HIM SAYS HE ABSORBS *SOLAR ENERGY* AND RETURNS IT AS FIERY *PLASMA BLASTS*--

--BUT, IF I ANGLE MY CLAWS TO *REFLECT* THAT ENERGY *BACK* AT HIM--

--I CAN *FRY* FLYBOY IN HIS OWN *JUICE*.

...THEN THERE'S THE GERMAN CIRCUS CLOWN WHO CALLS HIMSELF *NIGHTCRAWLER*...

I HOPE I CAN BE OF *HELP*, MEIN HERREN.

WITH *YOUR* POWERS, WAGNER-- *DEFINITELY*.

KID'S *SPRY*, BUT WHAT MAKES HIM *DANGEROUS* IS HIS ABILITY TO *TELEPORT*...

THING IS, I'VE NOTICED THE FAINTEST SCENT OF *SULPHUR* IN THE AIR AT THE SPOT WHERE HE'S ABOUT TO *MATERIALIZE*--

--SO I CAN HAVE A LITTLE *SURPRISE* WAITING TO TAKE HIM OUT OF THE GAME.

DREAMS BRIGHTEN

FABIAN NICIEZA
WRITER

SALVADOR LARROCA
ARTIST

TOM ORZECHOWSKI
LETTERER

DAVID OCAMPO
COLORIST

DO YOU FEEL WELL ENOUGH TO *TELEPORT* WITH ME?

YES, YES...IS THAT *WARREN?* ALWAYS RUSHING AWAY ON BUSINESS...

WHAT IS THAT...? IT LOOKS... FAMILIAR.

...?

PEOPLE ALWAYS WEAR *SHI'AR EXOSKELETON* FOR TELEPORTING.

COME, ERIK. *HANK* AND *REED* ARE WAITING FOR US IN NEW YORK.

"WE OFFERED THE WORLD A BETTER OPTION.

"WE OFFERED HOPE AND TRUTH, OPPORTUNITY AND ACCOMPLISHMENT."

THIRTY YEARS AGO WHEN MAGNETO AND I AVERTED A *NUCLEAR SHOWDOWN* BETWEEN THE UNITED STATES AND THE U.S.S.R.--

--WE MADE OUR *MUTANT ABILITIES* AND OUR DESIRE TO USE THEM FOR *GOOD* KNOWN TO THE ENTIRE WORLD.

WE SHOWED YOU THEN--AND HAVE TRIED TO SHOW YOU EVERY DAY SINCE THEN--

--THAT WHAT MATTERS MOST IS NOT *HAVING* POWER, BUT IN *HOW* THAT POWER IS USED.

ERIK...? ARE YOU ALL RIGHT?

THOSE WORDS, HANK-- THEY'RE SO FAMILIAR--LIKE AN *ECHO*...

...A PARADISE...

NO!!

HE HEARS THEIR PANIC.

PROFESSOR-- WHAT DID YOU *DO* TO HIM?

THE PAIN IN THE VOICES OF HIS STUDENTS, THEIR FEAR...

--I'M *BARELY* ABLE TO KEEP LOGAN'S BODY FROM *FALLING APART* AS IT IS!

THE VISION OF THE LIVES THEY *SHOULD* HAVE HAD--

--DISSIPATES LIKE FOG AND THE *REALITY* OF HIS ACTIONS SET IN.

CHARLES XAVIER HAS *DESTROYED* THE *MIND* OF THE MAN WHO WAS ONCE HIS *FRIEND.*

IN THE NAME OF *PEACE,* HE HAS COMMITTED A *BARBARIC* ACT.

AND THROUGH THE *GUILT,* HE CAN ONLY WONDER: WHAT PRICE WILL THEY ALL PAY FOR THE DECISION HE HAS MADE THIS DAY?

AS SILENCE SETTLES, ONE CAN ALMOST HEAR...

...THE FADING OF A DREAM...

END

ALL-NEW X-MEN #18 VARIANT

BY STUART IMMONEN, WADE VON GRAWBADGER & MARTE GRACIA

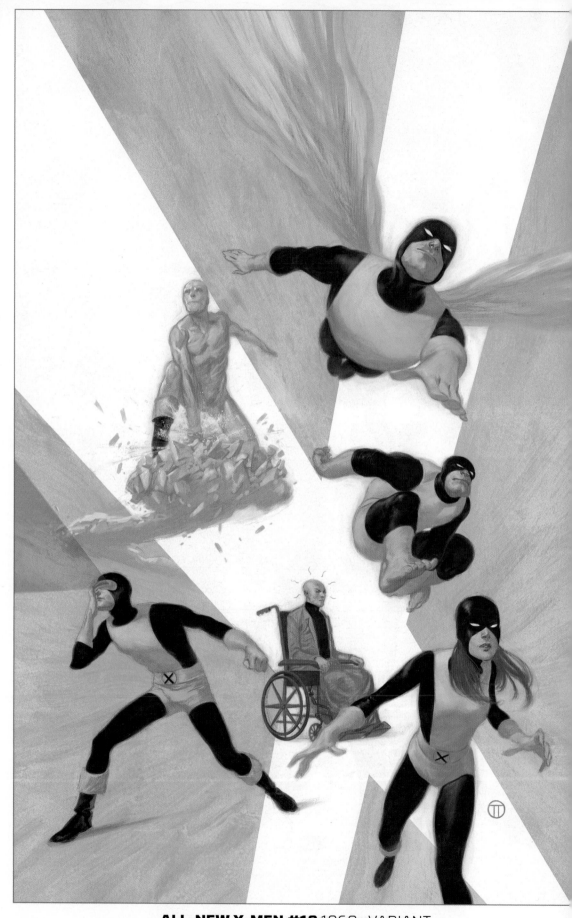

ALL-NEW X-MEN #18 1960s VARIANT
BY JULIAN TOTINO TEDESCO

ALL-NEW X-MEN #18 1970s VARIANT
BY JULIAN TOTINO TEDESCO

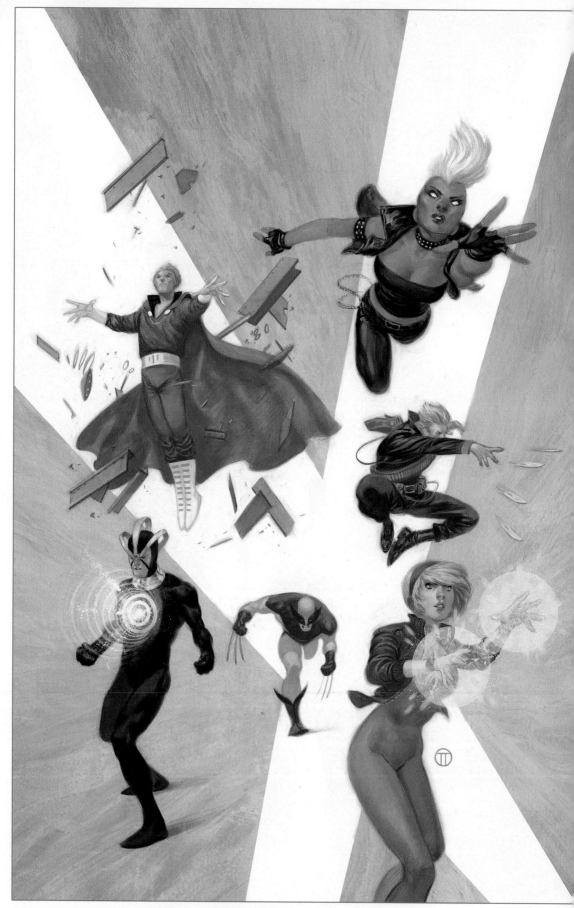

ALL-NEW X-MEN #18 1980s VARIANT
BY JULIAN TOTINO TEDESCO

ALL-NEW X-MEN #18 1990s VARIANT
BY JULIAN TOTINO TEDESCO

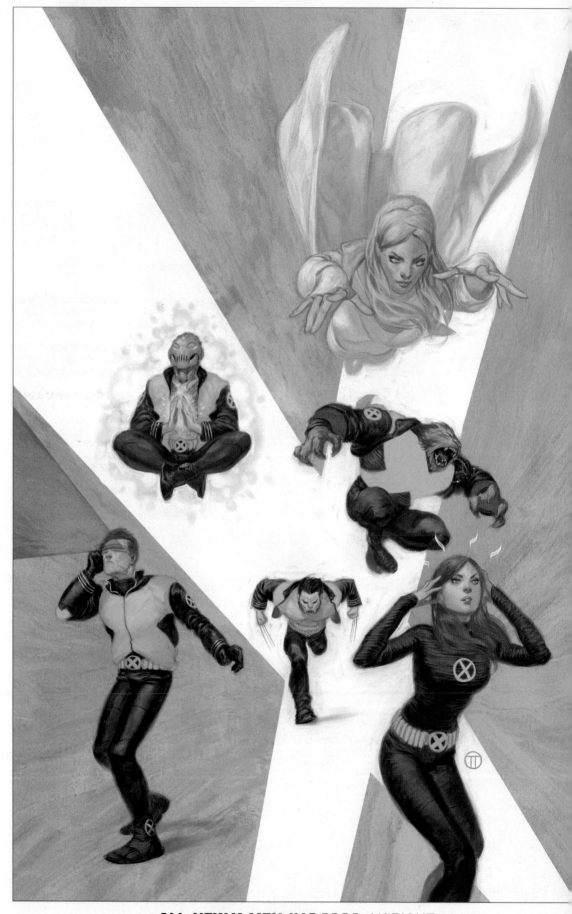

ALL-NEW X-MEN #18 2000s VARIANT
BY JULIAN TOTINO TEDESCO

THE TWELVE X-MEN 50TH
ANNIVERSARY VARIANT
COVERS INTERLOCK TO
FORM A GIANT POSTER.

LEFT TO RIGHT,
TOP TO BOTTOM:

SAVAGE WOLVERINE #6
BY WALTER SIMONSON
& JASON KEITH

WOLVERINE #11
BY DAVID LÓPEZ &
MORRY HOLLOWELL

ALL-NEW X-MEN #20
BY ARTHUR ADAMS
& JASON KEITH

ALL-NEW X-MEN #7
BY NICK BRADSHAW
& JASON KEITH

UNCANNY X-MEN #10
BY NEAL ADAMS &
DAVID CURIEL

UNCANNY X-FORCE #12
BY PHIL NOTO

ALL-NEW X-MEN #6
BY CHRIS BACHALO
& TIM TOWNSEND

CABLE AND X-FORCE #8
BY WHILCE PORTACIO,
CAM SMITH &
ANDRES MOSSA

UNCANNY X-FORCE #11
BY SALVADOR LARROCA
& FRANK D'ARMATA

ALL-NEW X-MEN #8
BY STUART IMMONEN,
WADE VON GRAWBADGER
& MARTE GRACIA

X-MEN #1
BY JOE MADUREIRA
& JASON KEITH

**WOLVERINE & THE
X-MEN #33**
BY CLAY MANN
& DAVID CURIEL

POSTER TOUCH-UP
COLORING BY
JASON KEITH

X-MEN: GOLD #1 VARIANT

BY JOHN CASSADAY & LAURA MARTIN